SOCIAL MEDIA SECRETS & STRATEGIES FOR EBAY SUCCESS

TWEET EYE TRAINING ACADEMY

VOLUME 3 / EDITION 1

BY THE DESIGNERS OF TWEET EYE SOFTWARE

www.tweet-eye.com

Copyright © 2015 Tweet Eye Limited

All rights reserved.

ISBN-10: 1516922182
ISBN-13: 978-1516922185

CONTENTS

1	MY EBAY STORY FORGET YOUR ASSUMPTIONS - DIRECTOR OF TWEET EYE'S STORY	4-7
2	THE ODDS ARE AGAINST SUCCESS	8-10
3	WHY MOST AMATEURS ARE RUBBISH AT MAKING EBAY PROFIT	11-12
4	YOU ARE NOT ALONE - JOIN LINKEDIN	13
5	FIVERR - AFFORDABLE PROFESSIONAL SERVICES TO HELP YOUR EBAY BUSINESS	14
6	USE YOUR EBAY SKILLS ON FIVERR TO HELP OTHER EBAYERS	15-18
7	YOUTUBE - PRIORITIZE YOUR TIME!	19
8	MISPLACED ASSUMPTIONS ABOUT EBAY SUCCESS	20-21
9	YOU NEED TO GEEK UP TO GET TRAFFIC	22-25
10	HASHTAGGING	26-31
11	REDEFINING THE OPPORTUNITIES ON EBAY	32-35
12	MARKETING PHRASES FOR SUCCESSFUL SOCIAL SELLING	36-40
13	MAKING MONEY WITH TWEET EYE	41-42

1 MY EBAY STORY - FORGET YOUR ASSUMPTIONS - DIRECTOR OF TWEET EYE'S STORY

Before the **Tweet Eye Training Academy** can help you achieve success on eBay I need to show you assumptions that can lead to failure.

Most people reading this book will have the same assumptions as I did that a successful eBay business begins by being built in a certain way.

I once purchased a book for thirty pence at a charity shop. I knew it was a good book and a quick search of the title of the book on bookfinder.com from my mobile phone proved my theory that I could retail the book for a lot higher than I purchased it for. I walked into the charity shop and purchased the book. ***I knew I could buy low and sell high.***

I paid some money to list it on eBay with some of the fancier formatting and listing and I was extremely proud when I sold the book for £5, nearly £4 profit after eBay listing fees.

My euphoria however was short lived. In the morning I logged into my eBay to get the buyer's address so that I could post them the book, only to discover to my dismay I had not set up my eBay listing carefully enough and my buyer was in America! It depleted all my profit on this one transaction by sending them the book from the UK. Live and learn!

There are so many things to think about and do to make a profit online, and most people believe that in order to make money on the internet you have got to spend money, and lots of it! Have you? This book is designed to educate you on **using picture posts and hashtags as a free and useful strategy to bring customers to your eBay and other offers. It will also show you how to do it at a low cost so you can maximize your ROI (return on investment) when it comes to spending money on various Social Media apps and tools.**

One of the goals of **The Tweet Eye Training Academy Series** is to explain to people the various income streams with massive potential that are available and which most people may not have even been aware of before. This book will mainly focus on eBay seller strategies and tools.

My first assumption that lead to failure

I wrongly assumed that eBay would have a ready made market of excited buyers. This was not the case. I just received 1 bid. The book was worth triple the value that the buyer bid for it. Had there been a lot more eyes of other people interested in the book niche I could have made considerably more money, unfortunately those eyes weren't on eBay!

eBay is now allowing people to write **Buyer Guide Articles (Blogs) to encourage more interaction from interested niches**. It is definitely worth doing this if you are mostly selling items of interest to one particular kind of niche.

To write eBay guide http://www.ebay.co.uk/gds / http://www.ebay.com/gds

In a piece of research carried out by Hubspot over 972 marketing professionals **25% of marketing professionals now consider blogging to be of critical importance to their business**. Blogging is considered a better return on investment in time than direct mail which is very expensive and ineffective for new leads, telemarketing and trade shows. **62% of marketing professionals interviewed considered Social Media the next most important method for driving leads and sales.**

http://www.slideshare.net/HubSpot/the-2012-state-of-inbound-marketing-webinar

Top methods eBay sellers can use to promote their products are Company Blog, LinkedIn, Twitter, Facebook and YouTube. ==Tweet Eye== can be used to cross promote eBay products by driving traffic directly to eBay products, Company Blogs, LinkedIn, Facebook and YouTube.

WHAT IS TWEET EYE?

TWEET EYE is a software application that makes it REALLY EASY to put your eBay products and website photos/images into a single Tweet or scheduled Tweet campaign. This is the CORE FEATURE of and reason for using Tweet Eye. It saves hours and hours of time. Other core features are discussed in Chapter 13.

'==Just remember that each post should include a direct link for purchase, a compelling image or video, and a relevant hashtag. The Tweet Eye app simplifies this process.=='

http://www.sitepronews.com/2015/09/11/how-to-boost-sales-through-social-media-marketing/

SOCIAL MEDIA SECRETS & STRATEGIES FOR EBAY SUCCESS

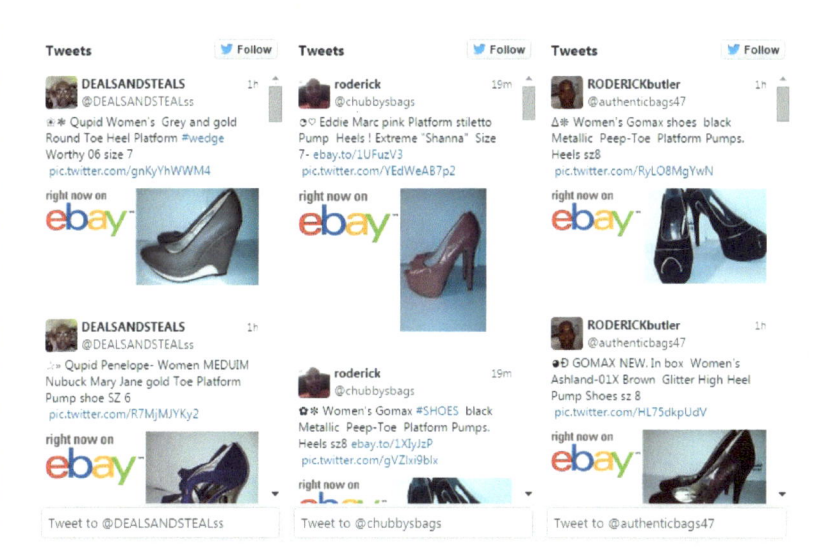

Testimonial of an eBay user promoting on Twitter using Tweet Eye

Hello Chris I'm loving the beta version my sales have doubled ... are you going to add other sites besides twitter like pinterest, google plus and tumbler. Thanks again

IMPROVE YOUR EBAY VIEWS FROM TWITTER TRY TWEET EYE TODAY

http://tweet-eye.com/

 ## 2. THE ODDS ARE AGAINST SUCCESS

With over $60 billion of goods sold a year on eBay (over $2,000 every second) eBay has so many rags to riches stories it is quite natural for any reader to try their hand at eBay too! It is natural for many people to feel disappointed when eBay success doesn't happen easily for them.

ARE YOU FED UP OF PAYING LISTING FEES AND NOT GETTING ENOUGH VIEWS TO MAKE SALES? YOU ARE NOT ALONE!

60% of eBay auctions don't result in a sale! Some categories of product sold on eBay have an even lower sell through rate.

http://www.quora.com/What-percentage-of-items-on-eBay-fail-to-sell

Sellers on eBay are doing everything they can to study eBay search formulas and monopolize top spots. Frankly your chances as new kid on the block are not good.

This book is designed to help you overcome the odds and find other opportunities to increase your eBay earnings.

Making money online can be very tough and that is why we put this book together to help you.

 **TOP TIPS TO BEAT THE ODDS**

How do you find the products that sell the most and study the sellers who are best at selling them?

How do you find market opportunities for the products that you already have?

Sites such as the ones below have already done the hard work for you.

1. You can find out which products have the best sell through rate at *Terapeak.com* eBay sellers also use tools such as *Terapeak.com* to help them to see market trends and find wholesalers to gage if they can buy items low and sell high.

2. Check out *Watchcount.com* to see which sellers get thousands of views daily. Study them carefully.

3. *Google Global Market Finder* offers some really useful insights into world demand for your items and you can this info for how you pitch it / hashtag your items on Social Media.

The Tweet Eye Training Academy

Test Google Global Market Finder today and be able to answer the following two questions about your business

1) How much your traffic would cost you if you were paying per click?

2) Which country is your product or service is searched for the most?

3) How many searches is your product getting a month?

Check out Watchcount.com today and be able to answer the following two questions about your business

1) When you search your product on Watchcount.com how many views is the top seller getting?

2) What can you learn from the top sellers presentation? ==SEE CHAPTER 12. MARKETING PHRASES FOR SUCCESSFUL SOCIAL SELLING==

Consider getting a subscription to Terapeak.com

3. WHY MOST AMATEURS ARE RUBBISH AT MAKING EBAY PROFIT

COST OF SALES How much money do you spend on items you plan to sell? How much time do you spend finding eBay items to sell? Do you spend money on petrol and transport? *I must have once spent an hour walking before I found that book in a local charity shop. I then drove home and spent another ten minutes of my time photographing and then listing the item.*

WHAT IF What happens if you pay out listing fees and don't get enough interested **VISITOR TRAFFIC** to sell your items? What happens if you pay for items and discover the market value is less than you paid for them?

EBAY IS NOT A READY MADE MARKET PLACE OF EXCITED BUYERS

Think of eBay more like a platform that helps facilitate the transaction between buyer and seller. The most successful sellers are those who do not rely solely on eBay to attract, market and sell their products.

The most successful sellers are the ones who put EFFORT into getting BUYERS to SEE their items.

Ask yourself what can you do to improve your profit margins?

Ask yourself what can you do to improve visitor traffic to your eBay? SEE CHAPTER 9. *YOU NEED TO GEEK UP TO GET TRAFFIC.*

4. YOU ARE NOT ALONE - JOIN LINKEDIN

 **LinkedIn forums for eBayers**
eBay Sellers - Official eBay Private Group

With over 10,000 members on LinkedIn the eBay Sellers - Official eBay Private Group offers perhaps some of the most useful insights by professional eBay members themselves on how to get ahead.

Most importantly the honest frustrations of sellers are discussed with experienced members giving ideas for work arounds.

 **JOIN TODAY**

https://www.linkedin.com/grp/home?gid=2710695

Try and ask at least one question on the LinkedIn forum about something that has been hindering your eBay sales. You may be very surprised at the response.

5. FIVERR - AFFORDABLE PROFESSIONAL SERVICES TO HELP YOUR EBAY BUSINESS

Fiverr.com is a website that every eBay seller should check out.

It is a website where all services and products sold start at just $5.

It offers really interesting opportunities for a person serious about making a career from eBay.

As a seller you can buy services which will give your eBay pages a profession look and finish. Perhaps you need a new logo or trying to find the right solution for drop shipping? Need a fixed price and high value service? FIVERR has the right experts ready to help you, and all for just $5!

On Fiverr you will find people willing to

- create amazing eBay store template
- list your items on eBay or Turbo Lister
- promote your eBay in Tweets and Pinterest pages
- provide you with trusted wholesale lists for drop shipping
- teach you eBay traffic systems
- share their eBay selling tips
- send amazing software for eBay traffic
- provide eBay listing & account management
- import eBay product list in WordPress

Fiverr is also encouraging sellers to sell small gift items. Unlike eBay there is no listing fee.

6. USE YOUR EBAY SKILLS ON FIVERR TO HELP OTHER EBAYERS

If you have been trying to succeed at eBay for some time you are likely to have picked up some skills.

You might not have the 'whole picture' of how to succeed as an eBay seller, but no doubt you will have practiced plenty at certain skills to try and make your eBay business a success.

In your professional life you may have gained skills that you didn't even realize could help you make you an extra income from helping other eBay sellers.

HELP OTHER SELLERS STANDOUT FROM THE REST

Do you have graphic design skills? Maybe you have years of experience tinkering with your own eBay store templates? There are scores of graphic designers who have increased the market demand for their services simply by promoting themselves as having bespoke skills for the eBay market place and by offering to make amazing template designs for eBay stores and auctions.

If you have amazing online design skills and understand how to implement your designs into eBay stores and auctions start offering your services on Fiverr.com and aim them at eBay sellers.

The Tweet Eye Training Academy

SELLERS WANT TRAFFIC

Got a social media account? eBay sellers will be interested in paying you to promote their items on it. Many owners of social media accounts have used gig sites such as Fiverr to turn their well followed social media account(s) or blog(s) into an asset.

Some common giggs might include.

I will promote ,Tweets and Pinterest your eBay or Etsy Products to 100,0000 People for $5.

I will advertise your specialty store at Etsy, eBay and/or Amazon to 112,000 Twitter followers interested in art design fashion beauty and more for $5.

IF YOU HAVE WELL FOLLOWED SOCIAL MEDIA ACCOUNT(S) OR KNOW HOW TO BUILD FOLLOWINGS ON SOCIAL MEDIA ACCOUNTS START OFFERING YOUR SERVICES TO EBAY SELLERS CHECKING OUT FIVERR.COM

FAKE FOLLOWS From the fact that highly followed social media accounts can earn frequently from sellers looking to promote, this has given rise to a completely new business. People selling the service of creating fake follows to boost the follower number counts.

SELLERS WANT TO SAVE TIME

Are you confident with tools such as Turbo Lister, doing eBay account management and listings or knowing how to import eBay product lists into WordPress?

Maybe you haven't been selling a lot yourself but all of those skills listed above are skills that some sellers desire help with and are willing to pay others to do.

Start offering your account management and listing services on Fiverr.com

SELLERS WANT MARKET INTELIGENCE

Do you know how to find market intelligence for selling using Terapeak.com / Watchcount.com / Google Global Market Finder ? Turn it into a service.

Offer a service / create a gigg on Fiverr that helps sellers understand the opportunities in their market.

SELLERS WANT ITEMS THEY CAN BUY AND SELL AT A PROFIT

Do you have a reliable list of drop shippers? On Fiverr you will find giggs like the ones below.

I will give over 990 best and trusted wholesalers list to drop shipping on eBay for $5.
I will help you find REAL wholesalers for $5.

Maybe you have a list to sell or system to teach people better drop shipping?

SELLERS WANT EASY WAYS TO PROMOTE THEMSELVES

Has this book taught you anything worth sharing? Having you got a lot of useful information about social media applications that will help sellers promote themselves?

Sellers want easy ways to promote themselves. Compile a list of useful social media services and sell the knowledge as a Fiverr Gigg.

IF YOU SUCCEED IN PROMOTING YOUR SERVICE FOR EBAYERS ON FIVERR THERE ARE HUNDREDS OF OTHER EMERGING GIGG WEBSITES! OFFER YOUR SERVICE ON OTHER PLATFORMS.

7. YOUTUBE - PRIORITIZE YOUR TIME

YouTube offers special opportunities particularly if your eBay items / stock is something you can demonstrate (e.g. a very successful seller of Magic Tricks on eBay uses YouTube videos to drive interest to their product).

YouTube is also a wonderful resource to learn solutions to link your eBay to Social Media.

You are very likely to get confused by looking at all the get rich quick eBay secrets on YouTube.

8. MISPLACED ASSUMPTIONS ABOUT EBAY SUCCESS

People assume they always have to go out and physically get items to buy low and sell high. This is not always the case.

Selling without buying first One business model is **drop shipping** - you do not buy items until someone has purchased them from you (drop shipping can be studied at **DSDomination.com**). Another alternative is **affiliate marketing** (**ebaypartnernetwork.com**) which allows you to make commissions while promoting the products of other businesses.

People assume they always have to pay fancy listing fees or be highly ranked in eBay Cassini search formulas to increase eBay traffic!

Some people assume the only route to success in eBay is spending more on listing fees or finding new ways to rank higher in eBay searches. **The trick is finding free or low cost ways to promote your products or services.** See Chapter 10 on the using hashtags and Chapter 13 on using Tweet Eye.

While many eBay sellers are working out where they stand with eBay's Cassini search introduced in 2015 or the next eBay search algorithm that eBay chooses to replace it, the odds are stacked against most sellers. There is so much competition and there are winners and losers in the eBay search algorithms. Some people assume the only route to success in eBay sales is to rank higher in eBay Cassini searches. This ignores the huge potential of **TRAFFIC** you can drive for free from other sources.

While eye catching listings certainly help you to standout on eBay each listing feature you purchase eats into your profits. There is huge potential **TRAFFIC** you can drive to your eBay for free from other sources.

Although eBay is a colossal sized business with over 112 million buyers and sellers using the platform, with many sellers competing for the attention of the potential buyers on the platform. The traffic you will directly gain from eBay search engine or attention grabbing listings is insignificant in size to the traffic you can drive yourself directly from social media.

The Tweet Eye Training Academy would like to teach you simple and powerful traffic driving methods which will greatly increase your relevant FREE visitor traffic to your eBay offers.

How big is the opportunity?

Twitter currently has over 292 million active users.

Defining colossal opportunity!

Facebook has over 1.2 billion users. If you compared Facebook membership to the number of people in countries of the world, Facebook would be the 3rd largest country in the world.

By not finding methods to connect your eBay promotions to social media posts, you are ignoring the opportunity to be seen by the largest online populations.

Tumblr has speculated 30 -50 million unique monthly users

Instagram has over 150 million users

Google+ has over 540 million active users

Pinterest has over 45 million users

9. YOU NEED TO GEEK UP TO GET TRAFFIC

==The most dangerous assumption you can make about the survival of your eBay business is that eBay will deliver you ALL the TRAFFIC you need for your eBay business to survive!==

GEEK UP or **GIVE UP.** If you have chosen to be in the business of online selling then you need online traffic.

When it comes to getting most traffic online GEEKS RULE!

The huge opportunities that exist for you as eBay seller to get more views from Social Media are hidden in **3 SIMPLE TRENDS**

1. **Trending popularity of sharing photos on social media platform with hashtags** Facebook, QQ, Weibo Twitter, Pinterest, Instagram, Tumblr.

and

2. **Increasing popularity of eBay sellers using RSS feed services to link their eBay RSS feeds to social media.** Twitterfeed.com, Google Feed Burner, Dlvr.it

and

3. **Increase of software and applications available to connect eBay sellers to Social Media** Including Tweet Eye

TO INCREASE ONLINE TRAFFIC THIS IS WHAT YOU NEED TO DO

1. Open up Social Media Accounts with Twitter, Facebook (Learn how to create a Facebook page)

2. Discover how to find your eBay RSS feed and use an RSS feed service such as Twitterfeed.com, Google Feed Burner, Dlvr.it to link your eBay RSS feed to your Social Media Accounts

RSS FEED SERVICES

You can also deliver new items from your eBay directly to social media using your eBay username RSS feed

Put this link into an RSS feed service such as http://twitterfeed.com/ to automatically update Facebook, Twitter, LinkedIn every time you add a new item

Put this link into an RSS feed service such as https://dlvr.it/ to automatically update Facebook, Twitter, Tumblr (and Google+ on paid subscription) every time you add a new item

To get even more views, use the advanced settings of the RSS feed services to prefix your updates with hashtags.

Most online RSS feed services are free to join, and are a very easy way to simultaneously post your updates to social media. Once set you can forget.

The Tweet Eye Training Academy

3. Learn how to choose hashtags and use Tweet Eye for automated posts to Twitter.

4. Learn how to link your Twitter Feed (now automated by Tweet Eye) to your Facebook page.

5. Learn how to make your Facebook page into an RSS feed and pass it through an RSS service into other social media networks e.g. Tumblr, LinkedIn other Twitter accounts, Facebook pages.

6. Learn about software and eBay apps that link your eBay offers to Social Media

APPS & SOFTWARE TO INCREASE TRAFFIC TO YOUR EBAY

http://tweet-eye.com/
http://apps.froo.com/pricing/app_description/?prefix=FSS
http://pagemage.com/
You can find even more solutions for your business at the eBay solutions directory.
http://cgi6.ebay.com/ws/eBayISAPI.dll?SolutionsDirectory

HOW GEEKING UP WITH SOCIAL MEDIA SKILLS CAN HELP YOU EARN FROM EBAY

Learning how to get traffic from social media will help you increase your eBay sales.

Learning how to get traffic from social media will help you increase your eBay affiliate sales.

Learning how to get traffic from social media will help you earn money from gigg websites such as Fiverr.

Learning how to get traffic from social media will help you design software and write books that other eBay businesses need and are willing to buy.

10. HASHTAGGING

THE SECRET OF HASHTAGGING

Hashtagging is about helping the millions of individuals who use social media networks research their niche and interests easily. With hundreds of millions of active social network users regularly clicking on hashtags of interest to them all you need to do is regularly Tweet relevant hashtags for your affiliate or sales offers.

HASHTAGS AS AN INDEX

Learn from the librarian, supermarket shelf stacker, fisherman; Approach Twitter and hashtagging in the same way a librarian would set about to **index** books in a library. Twitter is open for business and there are 500 million people searching for something so make sure they can find that something!

HASHTAGS ARE USED AS A EASY WAY TO HELP PEOPLE FIND THINGS

You must approach Twitter and Hashtagging in the same way a shelf stacker in a supermarket puts **everything in the correct**

place before the supermarket opens its doors to crowds of people looking for items they want. **People may not always come to buy, but they always come to look!** Make sure your keywords are hashtagged!

HASHTAGS AS A BAIT

Approach Twitter and hashtagging in the same way a fisherman **sets the bait**. Do you want to catch millionaires? Research the richest zip codes and place names, link your hashtagging for Gold Bullion and Ferraris against those place names using affiliate codes directing to eBay sellers in those areas. Want to profit from football fans? Coin Collectors? Stamp Collectors? Research their interests and hashtag the keywords which will be frequently discussed in those sorts of circles on Twitter. If you want to attract buyers in a certain geographic area do the same tweet but add the various towns in that area. For instance, promoting your original ladies jewelry line in the New York area might include these tweets that focus on particular towns in New York:

original **#ladiesjewelry** unique designs **#silverandgold #whiteplains** NY
original **#ladiesjewelry** unique designs **#silverandgold #elmsford** NY
original **#ladiesjewelry** unique designs **#silverandgold #yonkers** NY
original **#ladiesjewelry** unique designs **#silverandgold #rye** NY
original **#ladiesjewelry** unique designs **#silverandgold #scarsdale** NY
original **#ladiesjewelry** unique designs **#silverandgold #thornwood** NY
original **#ladiesjewelry** unique designs **#silverandgold #purchase** NY

HASHTAGS AS SPAM?

As advised earlier #Don't #spam #with #hashtags. Use sparingly and respectfully. Twitter best practice recommends no more than 2 or 3 hashtags per tweet.

 **HASHTAGS HAVE POTENTIAL**

Why would Instagram or Pinterest free image sharing **networks which index with hashtags be valued in the billions of dollars**, if sharing images for free on Social Media that could potentially make YOU revenue and sales wasn't worth it?

 **CREATE A HASHTAG STRATEGY**

To build your 'Bread' & 'Butter' hashtagging strategy, **The Tweet Eye Training Academy** have come across what they feel can help you choose the right hashtag

 http://blog.instagram.com

1. Be specific - Choose specific tags that will help you connect with other like-minded people

2. Be relevant - Relevant tags will help you attract new followers who will take a genuine interest

3. Be observant - Pay attention to the other hashtags used in content that use the same tag as yours.

The Tweet Eye Training Academy recommends that you begin by looking no further than the key words and phrases that Google suggest, and are related keywords to your products or services.

USE GOOGLE TO RESEARCH FREQUENTLY SEARCHED WORDS FOR HASHTAGGING STRATEGY

Google is the most visited website in the world. Google is second to none when it comes to data intelligence and research. Use Google Global Market Finder to help you understand how information is searched in your niche and where it is searched.

A search of Google Global Market Finder - Gives you an idea of how many people are searching for your product and how much you would have to pay for each click if using a search engine rather than FREE hashtagging.

http://translate.google.com/globalmarketfinder/g/index.html?locale=en#ren_GB

The Tweet Eye Training Academy

Step 1 - Begin by making all the popular search terms into hashtags.

Description	Local Monthly Searches	Cost Per Click	Hashtag(s)
hydroquinone	27,100	$0.77	**#hydroquinone**
skin lightening cream	9,900	$1.17	**#skinlighteningcream #skin #lightening #cream**
skin bleaching	9,900	$1.07	**#skinbleaching #skin #bleaching**

Using words and phrases suggested by Google in your marketing tweets and as hashtags makes you a very capable adversary of people already established on Twitter using a hashtag marketing strategy.

1) Every time a competitor hashtags their product or service they have now got to share their potential customer eyes with you.

2) Search engines may also pick up on the frequency of the relevant terms used in your Tweets and your online traffic will increase from search engines as well.

USE HASHTAG ANALYSIS SERVICES TO RESEARCH RELATED HASHTAGS

Step 2 - Use **Various Twitter analysis services available to help inspire you** to choose related words and hashtags and analyse the reach of each tag you use.

Consider services such as

 Tweet-Eye.com

 Hashtagify.me

 Trendsmap.com

 Sopularity.com

 Ritetag.com

11. REDEFINING OPPORTUNITIES ON EBAY

There are many less conventional routes to make a profit from eBay. As director of Tweet Eye my route to eBay success has been a bit less conventional than that of most eBayers.

First of all **it is important to redefine eBay success.** eBay is a huge market place business which many businesses can make an income from meeting the needs of eBay sellers. In chapter 6 the Tweet Eye Training Academy introduced you to a few ideas of how you can start earning on Fiverr by offering to **USE YOUR EBAY SKILLS ON FIVERR TO HELP OTHER EBAYERS**

eBay is a network of over 112 million sellers in a global economy where everyone is desperate to sell at a profit opens up huge opportunities.

BUILDING A SUCCESSFUL EBAY CAREER WITHOUT INVENTORY TO SELL ON EBAY

The most helpful thing you can do for other eBay sellers and also earn yourself money (a commission from eBay) for doing it, is become an eBay affiliate.

You don't need to own any items to sell yourself, you just need to become an expert at getting traffic to other people's items using commissionable links from the eBay Partner Network.

This is how my own path to success started. I was so despondent with the risk of buying items at one price and selling at virtually no profit after listing fees and postage the first opportunity I explored was being an eBay affiliate.

Being an eBay affiliate was an easy way of selling anything I wanted online without risking my own money to buy stuff.

==In April 2013 'eBay Partner Network' gave permission to all of its affiliates to make posts to Twitter and Facebook, massively==

==increasing the opportunities for affiliates to earn money from social media posts.==

You would be amazed at what products I have managed to sell for other eBayers simply by posting images of their items with hashtags to Social Media.

In my first few months as an eBay affiliate I decided to promote common products most people use. I successfully increased affiliate income from promoting shoes, shoes, more shoes, some wedding dresses, engagement rings, etc.

Then I got ambitious and started tweeting eBay commissionable links with pictures of toys, cars, and speed boats.

Next, I started tweeting eBay commissionable links with pictures of gold bullion, bitcoin and snow mobiles. Testing my theories even further I tweeted eBay commissionable links of dinosaur poo and earned eBay commissions.

As an eBay affiliate I quickly learned that there were over 18,000 categories to market from on eBay.com alone (there are many eBay sites and languages).

I learned the simple challenge as an affiliate was to help buyers and sellers of any nation meet, simply by researching what one nation has got to sell and what another nation is looking for most. Posting photos of items in tweets and using hashtags helped link people browsing Twitter to eBay seller promotions and my income as an affiliate began to grow.

Then something terrible happened for eBay affiliates, the eBay partner network changed the goal post of how they rewarded eBay affiliates commissions. As an affiliate I was still helping sellers to sell more, by connecting buyer to seller via social media, but eBay was paying me as an affiliate less for doing it!

So I stopped tweeting affiliate offers simply for the sake of tweeting them and specific sellers would pay me to Tweet for them. I was effectively getting paid by sellers on eBay for the time I would have spent doing random tweet promotions as an affiliate!

> Another system people try to make money from eBay is DSDomination.com
>
> DSDomination.com is a system that teaches people how to find items on Amazon and resell them for a profit on eBay.com

TWEET EYE SOFTWARE WAS ORIGINALLY DEVELOPED FOR EBAY USERS, BUT ITS APPLICATION HAS NOW EXPANDED

Such was the demand and desperation of more eBay sellers wanting traffic to promote their items, I realized that there was a need to develop Tweet Eye. Tweet Eye is a tool that helps eBay sellers (as well as Etsy sellers and independent websites) tweet their photos to Twitter and it had over 2,000 downloads in its first year! Its strength lies in its ease of use, the ability to capture pictures/images and then tweet them out on an automated schedule. It literally saves hours and hours of time in tweeting.

12. MARKETING PHRASES FOR SUCCESSFUL SOCIAL SELLING

 **THE POWER OF WORDS**

CHANGE YOUR WORDS AND CHANGE YOUR WORLD

BECOMING A SUCCESSFUL MARKETER IS AS SIMPLE AS

ONE, TWO, THREE

MOST LIKELY YOU PURCHASED THIS BOOK BECAUSE WE USED WORDS SUCH AS **SUCCESSFUL** …. **SECRET**

Learn how language influences emotions and persuades action. Play on emotional triggers with words and phrases and you will increase your success.

Many marketers follow a simple three stage formula for constructing perfect marketing phrases.

1. Identify your customer need or problem (PAIN)

We knew that our 'customers' eBay sellers always think they are not selling enough (that is our customer's pain). We created a catchy title to identify with that pain.

What is your customer need or pain?

Are you selling chairs? A customer does not need a chair, they need a comfortable place to sit!

2. Give them the solution (SOLUTION)

The Tweet Eye Training Academy

The title promised solutions

Do your eBay descriptions give solutions?

3. Tell them to do it (CALL TO ACTION)

    Got bad breath?   (PAIN)
    Clean your teeth.   (SOLUTION)
    Do it now!   (CALL TO ACTION)

Our marketing tweets and social media posts are likely to use call to action words such as 'Buy it now','Discover now','Don't delay'

Below are some other powerful ideas for words from **verticalresponse.com** that will make a difference.

Write as though you're speaking to people

YOU

Give people a reason why they need to take action.

BECAUSE

Nobody wants to miss a FREE deal

FREE

People love VALUE

VALUE

minimize concerns of risk

GUARANTEED

People love to be amazed!

AMAZING

Make it simple for people to take the next step

EASY

Make people curious

DISCOVER

Motivate people to respond immediately to a

Limited-time offer.

ACT NOW

This establishes that your product or service is all people will need to buy in order to achieve their goal.

EVERYTHING YOU NEED

Point out a "negative benefit," such as "never worry again" or "never overpay again."

NEVER

Your product or service is the cutting edge in your industry.

NEW

The most powerful word to showcase monetary savings, or even time savings.

SAVE

Remind customers that your product, service or business is tried-and-true.

PROVEN

"Proven" to minimize risk perception for health and monetary loss.

SAFE AND EFFECTIVE

Let customers know that your business, product or service is robust.

POWERFUL

Not everyone succeeds, and there are secrets to success. Let customers know you can reveal those secrets.

SECRET

Because customers want a great deal, remember?

BARGAIN

Create a win-win situation for your customers.

NO OBLIGATION

Start off with a solution so customers read the rest of your copy.

HOW TO

It is no secret that words are powerful in influencing actions. There are proven strategies to use words to give you more effective results.

Learn as much as you can about how to use the right words in the right way. Check out more suggestions at

http://www.verticalresponse.com/blog/the-30-magic-marketing-words/

13. MAKING MONEY WITH TWEET EYE

For the last two years the **Tweet Eye Training Academy,** have been steadily increasing their income every year simply from sending great photos with hashtags to Twitter.

The **Tweet Eye Training Academy** have used many of the ideas discussed in this book to create businesses using pictures along with smart hashtagging covered in **#Hashtag Your Way To The Top**, to boost the visibility of those businesses on Twitter and increase sales.

Understanding the full potential of using pictures in social media posts containing hashtags will considerably raise the interest you get in your business in future years, as social media becomes more and more the primary way of reaching new business online. Tweet Eye was created with this goal in mind and to provide a simple automated solution.

WHAT IS TWEET EYE?

TWEET EYE is a software application that makes it REALLY EASY to put your eBay products and website photos/images into a single Tweet or scheduled Tweet campaign. This is the CORE FEATURE of and reason for using Tweet Eye. It saves hours and hours of time.

Currently, some of its core features are:

AUTOMATION – Tweets with pictures can be set to go out at intervals of between thirty minutes and 24 hours (or even on a random setting). The scheduled tweets can go on for weeks or even months until you cancel or revise them.

TWEET WITH PICTURES EFFORTLESSLY – The software requires you to enter the url you want to promote and brings up the pictures/images from that url. Then you click on the picture or image you want included in your tweet, type in your tweet, choose your hashtags and click "OK".

FREE VERSION – Currently there is a free version available. Silver, Gold and Platinum fee based versions will be released with an estimated launch date of October 1, 2015.

HASHTAG ANALYSIS – For those of you with writer's block the fee based versions will also have a hashtag analysis function to help improve your tweeting.

EASY TO USE – It's so easy even a teenager can use it, just kidding. It's so easy even people over 50 can figure out how to use it . . . seriously!!!

MARKETING – Use Tweet Eye to promote your websites, blogs, social media pages, Etsy and eBay products. (Note: Our testing shows Tweet Eye works with the great majority of websites we have tested.)

We hope you will enjoy the series and other resources of the Tweet Eye brand.

Please feel free to write to us at contact@tweet-eye.com

Also, check out our blog at http://tweet-eye.com/news.htm

The Tweet Eye Training Academy wish you every success!

The Tweet Eye Training Academy

RECOMMENDED READING

#Hashtag Your Way To The Top

Picture Yourself @ The Top

www.ingramcontent.com/pod-product-compliance
Lightning Source LLC
Chambersburg PA
CBHW040929180526
45159CB00002BA/670